Was it a W

A HANDY GUIDE TO
THE MARINE MAMMALS
OF THE HEBRIDES

by
Jay Butler & Anna Levin

The idea for this booklet grew from the series of records that have been kept in the bookshop in Tobermory on the Isle of Mull since 1977. The steady stream of people over the years who came in to report their sightings were excited by what they had seen but generally found precise description and positive identification very difficult. What was needed was an identification guide which concentrated on the most common species and showed them as they are in the field - alive, elusive and moving through the water. How fortunate we were, then, to have Jay Butler and Anna Levin to put together this guide to the most common species to be seen in these waters. Jay Butler, after taking a degree in Neurobiology at the University of Sussex, was awarded her Ph.D. for behavioural studies on badgers, after which she worked on the IFAW's research vessel "Song of the Whale" in the Azores and became, as she says "completely fascinated by cetacean biology and never looked back!" Anna Levin, whose degree in Social Anthropology from Edinburgh University led to an interest in the interactions between cetaceans and humans, travelled half way round the world to look at whales and study whale-related tourism. Her passion for whales and dolphins took her to Ireland, the former Yugoslavia and New Zealand and the drawings in this book are a tribute to the acuteness of her observations. She and Jay came together when working for the Hebridean Whale and Dolphin Trust in Tobermory where we persuaded them to combine their expertise in this handy guide which has also benefited from the advice and patient proof-reading of Judith Misson.

You could not do better than take Jay and Anna with you on a whale-watching trip, if not in person, at least in the form of this little book.

Brown & Whittaker
Second edition 1999
Reprinted 2002

INTRODUCTION

The Hebrides hold a fascination that has long had the ability to entice naturalists to them. These magnificent islands, with their varied landscapes, copious wildlife and clear blue seas, possess a mystique that leaves one spellbound. The unpolluted shores that surround the Inner Hebridean islands are a haven for a remarkable diversity of wildlife and, in Britain, must surely be second to none. Whether you visit by land or sea, in summer or winter, a trip to the Hebrides is an experience not easily forgotten.

To eat lunch on a boat that is nestled in the turquoise shallows off the Cairns of Coll on a warm summer's day is like stealing a piece of heaven. The be-whiskered faces of seals will pop up and scrutinise their observers with large doleful eyes. The observer, staring back, will generally stop, mid-munch, and scrabble for the ever elusive camera. The silken bodies then roll over and disappear into the blue watery depths leaving one struggling to keep track of the fleeting shadows as they dart this way and that beneath the surface.

To have the chance to see the smooth, glassy, bodies of dolphins leap effortlessly from the water as they play alongside a boat, or watch the slow emergence of a minke whale's long, grey back as it breaks the water's surface is an experience that leaves one humbled and exalted.

In comparison with continental Europe, Britain's natural environment can be described as 'maritime'. In addition, as parts of the Hebrides extend beyond the continental shelf, the Western Isles, when compared with mainland Britain, can be described as oceanic. Generally people do not realise just how many of the 79 species of whale, dolphin and porpoise (collectively known as cetaceans) can be seen in these oceanic waters. This book is not intended to be an exhaustive catalogue of all these species nor is it an inventory of each marine mammal present in Hebridean waters. It is a simple guide designed to help the casual observer identify those mammals we believe are most likely to be encountered.

HOW TO USE THIS BOOK

If you see a black back or fin break the surface of the water, **don't** search frantically through the pages of this guide! Go straight to the 'model mammal' page at the back and try to run methodically through the questions, writing down everything you see. Get down as much information as you can while you have the animal in your sights, there will be plenty of time to search for a likely candidate when the animal has gone. The same principle applies to a dark figure scurrying along the shoreline. Note where it was seen, what it was doing and what size and shape it was. Then, when the animal has gone, compare your field notes with the guide and see if you can find an appropriate match.

Contents

Text and illustrations © Jay Butler and Anna Levin 1998

Published by Brown & Whittaker Publishing, Tobermory, Isle of Mull, PA75 6PR

Printed by Nevisprint, Fort William

ISBN 09528428 9 0

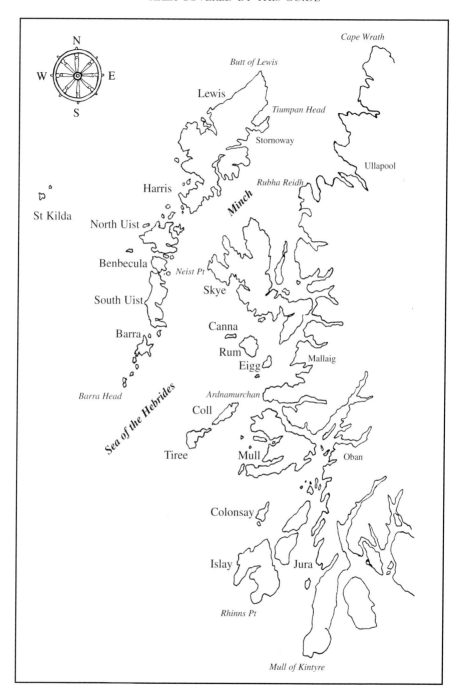

CETACEAN SPOTTING FROM LAND

General Hints & Tips:

What to take:

Always make sure that you have warm clothes and a waterproof as the weather can change rapidly. Take a flask with a hot drink and something to nibble on. Binoculars, with a magnification of between 7 and 10 times, are a MUST. Take a chinagraph pencil to jot down the salient features of your sighting on the model mammal on the back cover (e.g. fin size, position and shape, coloration etc). If you plan on spending the day in a remote location take a whistle and torch with you and tell someone where you are going and when you expect to return

Location:

The best places to try are usually headlands where you can gain some height. Generally speaking the higher you are the greater the distance over which observations can be made. However, if you are watching at sea level don't forget to use your ears. The sound of a blow can be quite distinctive as indeed are the clicks, squeaks and whistles made by many of the dolphin species. Any areas of coastline that overlook bays, inlets or islands are also good. Always keep your eyes peeled on ferry trips as they are an excellent platform from which to view all sorts of wildlife

Weather conditions:

Try to choose a calm, preferably overcast, day. As a general rule if you can see the familiar meringue-like white tips of foam as waves break then go home and try again another day. Cetaceans, especially the smaller ones, are difficult to see at the best of times and as one of the principal indicators of their presence is a disturbance of the surface, the calmer the water the better your chances of spotting a fin.

How to watch & what to look for:

Once comfortably settled in a suitable spot with sandwiches, flask and your well worn copy of *Was it a Whale*, start skimming the surface of the water initially with the naked eye. Make slow sweeps back and forth looking for any surface disturbance. As some cetaceans are known to associate with birds if you see a number of seabirds diving, circling or just sitting on the water's surface concentrate your binoculars in that area. If you think you have spotted a fin make sure to scan the area surrounding the sighting as well as the initial spot. Cetaceans may remain below the surface for some time so keep scanning the area for a good few minutes. Try and note the direction of travel and then scan ahead of the point last seen.

When to watch:

Although cetaceans can be watched at any time of day the best light conditions are generally first thing in the morning (two or three hours after dawn) or late in the afternoon (one or two hours before sunset). Some of the smaller cetaceans (porpoises and dolphins) are known to be most active in the two hours after and before high water so if you are watching in an area with tidal currents be especially vigilant during those times.

The following is a small selection of 'hot spots' throughout the Hebrides where, with patience, binoculars and a little luck you should have a good chance of seeing a cetacean. If you discover any hot spots of your own please let us know.

Colonsay

OS Map reference: Landranger 60

In addition to some dolphin species minke whales have been sighted from both Rubha Dubh and Rubh' A' Geodha.

Islay

OS Map reference: Landranger 60

Keep your eyes peeled on any ferry trip to or from the island as cetaceans are regularly spotted from the Kennacraig ferry on both the Port Askaig and the Port Ellen routes. Dolphins, porpoises, minke whales and even killer whales have been sighted from the Rubh' a' Mhail lighthouse on the northern tip of the island. Almost any position along the west coast where you can gain a little altitude to look down onto the Sound of Islay is a good place to try as many different species are regularly seen along this stretch of water. Follow the A847 south through the Rhinns of Islay until you come to Rhinns point where you can park at the pub. From here you can walk along the coast north to Ruba na Faing or south down to Rhinns Point. This entire stretch is excellent for cetacean sighting and has views across the ocean that defy description. For those who fancy cetacean spotting from an easy chair try the hotel at Port Charlotte which looks out over Loch Indaal. Just a little further north along Loch Indaal is Bruichladdich pier which is another good spot for those who don't fancy long walks and exhausting climbs.

Lewis

OS Map reference: Landranger 8 13 & 14

The Eye Peninsula (Point) on the Isle of Lewis provides excellent headlands for viewing cetaceans. The best spot is Tiumpan Head on the end of the peninsula (11m from Stornoway, accessible by car and bus). At 100 feet Tiumpan Head is an excellent height for viewing a large area of sea. To the left of this headland is Broad Bay which is a hotspot for harbour porpoises. Groups of 20+ porpoises have been seen foraging in the bay. Looking north and to the right of the headland into the Minches, Risso's dolphins can be seen very close inshore and often pass around the headland just below the cliffs. White-beaked dolphins and minke whales are also sighted here. The white-beaked dolphins prefer deeper water and are usually a little way out from the shore but with good binoculars are quite easy to find. Look for a small group size. The occasional killer whale has also been sighted here. Branahuic Bay, just five minutes from Stornoway, seems to be an important social area for Risso's dolphins and (especially during August and October), you may see large groups engaged in elaborate displays of breaching and tail slapping.

Jura

OS Map reference: Landranger 61

Almost anywhere along the north end of the sound of Jura is good for cetacean spotting although may require some strenuous walking. Take the A846 northbound until you reach Inverlussa then walk east to Lussa point. From here there are numerous footpaths to choose from which take you through stupendously rugged and beautiful terrain. Whether you choose to follow the coast up to the north-east or down to the south-west your chances of seeing cetaceans are good. If you are up to a decent climb, excellent sightings (binoculars essential) can be obtained from Beinn Sgaillinish just north of Tarbert.

Mull

OS Map reference: Landranger 47 & 48

Rubha nan Gall (Tobermory) lighthouse, Salen, and Grasspoint are good spots to view harbour porpoises. Bottlenose dolphins are occasionally sighted from Calgary Bay and Grasspoint. It is also worth taking binoculars up to the masts above Cnoc Fuar Cottage on the Glengorm estate as both minke whales and bottlenose dolphins can sometimes be seen in the channel towards Drimnin and north towards the island of Coll. On the south of the island try Loch Buie, and the Iona ferry.

Rum

OS Map reference: Landranger 39

On the north shores of the island, close to Kilmory cottage, common dolphins may be seen. The shores of Harris, on the west are also worth a visit and may provide sightings of dolphins, minke whales and perhaps even a killer whale. Otters are common along almost all the coastal areas and many of the lochs and rivers of the island. On the north side of the island, Kilmory bay and Samhnan Insir are good places to try and on the south, Loch Scresort. The Gaelic name for the south side shore is actually 'Carn an Dobhrain Bhig' which means Cairn of the little otter'

Skye

OS Map reference: Landranger 32

Try Neist Point on the extreme east of the island, and Kilt Rock on the west coast of Trotternish. Sightings of minke, killer whales and a variety of dolphins have been seen from here.

Mainland

As always, all the major headlands provide good viewing platforms. The lighthouses at Rubha Reidh (12 miles from the village of Gairloch) and Ardnamurchan are excellent locations for sighting a variety of dolphin species and basking sharks as well as killer, pilot and minke whales. From Ardnamurchan look out towards the Small Isles (Muck, Eigg and Rum) as minke whales often come here to feed during the summer months. If you spot a large gathering of birds there may well be a minke around.

If you fancy a day at sea then contact the local tourist office for details of the rapidly increasing number of wildlife boat trips which operate throughout the Hebrides.

HARBOUR PORPOISE
(Phocoena phocoena)

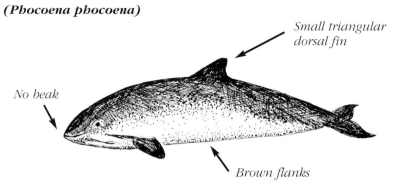

Small triangular
dorsal fin

No beak

Brown flanks

Length: 1.35-1.8m (4.5-5.9ft)

ID features: Very small with a dark grey back and brown flanks. The fin is insignificant and triangular in shape. As the individual surfaces movement tends to be circular as if the fin were fixed to a wheel revolving underwater.

Sound: May hear the blow, which comes out as a short sharp puff similar to a suppressed sneeze.

Group sizes: 1-20+

Typical behaviour: Elusive swimmers which are easily missed as only a small part of the back and fin are seen on surfacing. They are shy and will not usually approach boats. Extremely unlikely to be seen jumping clear of the water. Commonly sighted in coastal areas especially around headlands and estuaries with peak numbers occurring in March/April and from July to November.

Confused with: These animals have a distinct lack of characteristic markings and at distance are therefore easily confused with other small cetaceans.

BOTTLENOSE DOLPHIN
(Tursiops truncatus)

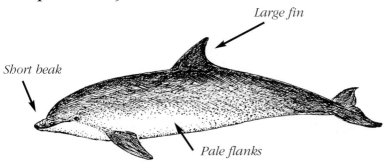

Large fin

Short beak

Pale flanks

Length: 2.2-4.0m (7.3-13.2ft)

ID features: Body is dark grey in colour with paler flanks and white underside but with an absence of distinctive markings. The fin is large and curved and the beak is short.

Sound: Clicks, squeaks and whistles may be heard.

Group sizes: Small groups 2-20+

Typical behaviour: Exuberant individuals whose chunky forms are often seen leaping out of the water (when the white underside may be seen). Will play around boats and bowride. Seen all year, but in coastal waters mainly July to October.

Confused with: Common and Atlantic white-sided dolphins, harbour porpoise. Bottlenose are bigger and less agile than either the common or white-sided dolphins and lack distinctive flank markings. At a distance, may be confused with the harbour porpoise but look for a noticeably larger size, active behaviour and a curved, as opposed to the triangular, fin.

COMMON DOLPHIN
(Delphinus delphis)

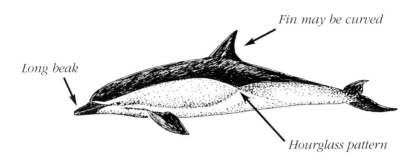

Fin may be curved

Long beak

Hourglass pattern

Length: 1.7-2.4 m (6-8ft)

ID features: Distinctive hourglass pattern of yellowish tan on side of the body becoming pale grey behind the dorsal fin which is centrally placed and may be curved or erect.

Sound: Very vocal species, clicks and whistles often clearly heard from a boat.

Group sizes: 10-100's

Typical behaviour: Very animated. Fast swimmers which, if they are not engrossed in feeding, love to bowride. Often seen jumping clear of the water. May sometimes be found associating with diving gannets. Seen May to September in coastal waters, most common in the Southern Hebrides.

Confused with: Similar to other dolphins at a distance but once the distinctive hourglass pattern is seen the animal is unmistakable.

KILLER WHALE
(Orcinus orca)

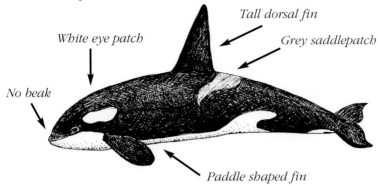

Tall dorsal fin

White eye patch

Grey saddlepatch

No beak

Paddle shaped fin

Length: 5.5-9.8 m (18-32 ft)

ID features: Distinctive, tall, centrally placed triangular dorsal fin sometimes tilted forward. In males the fin may reach 1.8m (the size of a fully grown man), smaller and more curved in females. Characteristic black and white coloration with white eye patches and a grey saddlepatch behind the dorsal fin. Large paddle shaped flippers.

Sound: Clicks and whistles. Sometimes a harsh scream may be heard.

Group sizes: 2-10+

Typical behaviour: Fast swimmers, rarely bowride, although can be quite inquisitive and playful. May jump clear of the water and slap their tails and or flippers against the surface of the water. Are sometimes seen chasing seals.

Confused with: These animals are BIG. The distinct black and white markings and, in the males, the colossal dorsal fin make the killer whale difficult to confuse with any other species. Females may be confused with bottle-nosed dolphins, Risso's or pilot whales. White patch diagnostic.

RISSO'S DOLPHIN
(Grampus griseus)

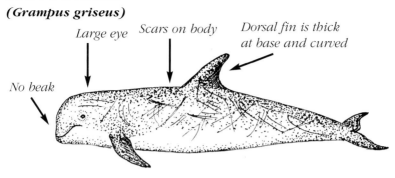

Large eye Scars on body Dorsal fin is thick at base and curved

No beak

Length: 2.6-3.8m (8.5 -12.5 ft)

ID features: Rotund individuals with a blunt rounded head and no beak. The dark grey back and flanks lighten with age until they become almost white. Scarring, which looks like white criss-cross lines, is seen on the bodies of older individuals. The dorsal fin is dark, large and thick at the base tapering slightly toward to tip. The tip tends to curve backward toward the tail.

Sound: Clicks and whistles may be heard also loud cracks as they slap their tails against the water's surface.

Group sizes: Usually 6-30+ although can be in 100's

Typical behaviour: Rarely bowride, but may accompany boats. Slow, graceful swimmers. Very active, and may be seen jumping clear of the water or slapping their tails against the water's surface. Can also sometimes be seen poking their noses out of the water and observing boats with a large, black eye. Usually seen near to the coastline, often around creel pots. May be seen in coastal waters mainly from May to September.

Confused with: Pilot whales but can be distinguished by the paler colouration, scarring and more animated behaviour.

STRIPED DOLPHIN
(Stenella coeruleoalba)

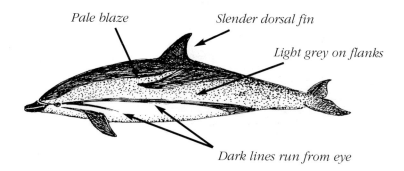

Pale blaze

Slender dorsal fin

Light grey on flanks

Dark lines run from eye

Length: 2-2.4m (6.2-8.3 ft)

ID features: Dark grey back with light grey on the flanks. Two characteristic dark lines, which may be seen at close quarters, may help to identify this species. Both run from the eye one extending to the flipper and the other to the tail region. They have a slender, curved fin.

Sound: Clicks, squeaks and whistles may be heard.

Group sizes: 10-500

Typical behaviour: Very spirited behaviour, when swimming at speed in large groups often seen jumping high and clear above the water. May be seen in deep coastal waters between July and December.

Confused with: Common dolphins, which are similar in shape and size, but the dark body stripe and absence of hourglass pattern should be sufficient to confirm the species type.

WHITE-BEAKED DOLPHIN
(Lagenorhynchus albirostris)

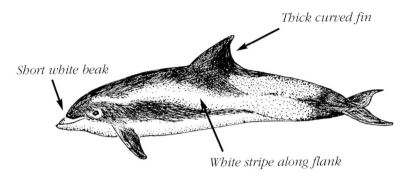

Thick curved fin

Short white beak

White stripe along flank

Length: 2.5-2.7m (8.2-8.9ft)

ID features: Short, white, stumpy beak with a large, thick, very curved fin. Dark grey in colour with a white stripe along the body which swirls upwards over the shoulder.

Sound: May hear squeaks, clicks, and sometimes also the explosive sound of a tail being slapped against the water's surface.

Group sizes: Usually small groups 4-10 animals although larger groups of 50+ are seen.

Typical behaviour: Often bowride although they usually lose interest after a few minutes. Sometimes seen jumping clear of the water and may slap tail against surface. Generally found in the deeper waters of central and northern North Sea but also in Atlantic, in coastal waters of North Hebrides.

Confused with: Similar to other species of dolphin, especially the Atlantic white-sided dolphin (see opposite). Look at the colour of the stripes on the flank. In the white beaked these are all white or grey whereas the white-sided have either a yellow or tan coloured stripe. When bowriding the white beak is easy to see.

ATLANTIC WHITE-SIDED DOLPHIN
(*Lagenorhynchus acutus*)

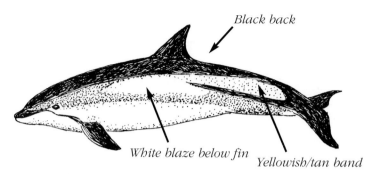

Black back

White blaze below fin

Yellowish/tan band

Length: 2.0-2.8m (6.6-9.2ft)

ID features: Black on back with a yellowish/ tan band on the flanks broken by a distinctive white blaze which runs below the dorsal fin. Large, centrally placed, curved dorsal fin.

Sound: Squeaks and clicks may be heard.

Group sizes: Offshore usually large groups of 100's, although smaller groups of 20+ are seen inshore.

Typical behaviour: Active at the surface, fast swimmers which occasionally bowride although not as much as common dolphins. May be seen leaping clear of water when travelling. Peak numbers are seen in coastal waters from July to September.

Confused with: White-beaked and common dolphins. The white-sided lacks the common dolphin's hourglass pattern along the flank. To differentiate between white-beaked and white-sided, look for the number of pale/white stripes. White-beaked dolphins have two stripes whereas white-sided have only one.

MINKE WHALE
(Balaenoptera acutorostrata)

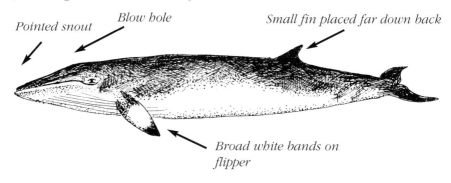

Pointed snout

Blow hole

Small fin placed far down back

Broad white bands on flipper

Length: 7-10m (23-33ft)

ID features: The head is pointed, triangular and deeply ridged and the back is dark grey or black with a pale underside. The flippers have distinctive broad white bands which are clearly visible when viewed at close quarters. The fin, which is situated two thirds of the way down the back, is small, thick at the base and curved.

Group sizes: Singular or in groups, occasionally up to 10.

Typical behaviour: Often seen with seabirds, especially when feeding which it does by breaking through the surface of the water with a gaping mouth. The indistinct vertical blow can be heard but is seldom seen. The long, dark, smooth back can be seen rolling through the water. The tail is not seen above the surface. If close enough to detect it the blow has a delightful smell of rotting cabbage! May be inquisitive about boats. Normally 3-5 short dives before a longer period of 5-10 minutes. Usually seen in coastal waters from May-October.

Confused with: Pilot whales at a distance but can usually be distinguished by the fin and head shape. Also look for the white bands on the flippers and try to note the characteristic dive sequence.

LONG-FINNED PILOT WHALE
(Globicephala melas)

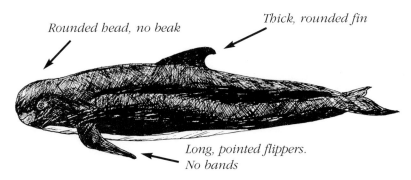

Rounded head, no beak

Thick, rounded fin

*Long, pointed flippers.
No bands*

Length: Males are 5-6m (12-19ft) Females are smaller than males.

ID features: Chunky body with a blunt bulbous head and no beak. The dorsal fin is long, thick at the base and rounded backwards at the tip. Uniformly dark skin except for a white anchor shaped patch on the chin. Powerful blow (1m) which is clearly visible in calm conditions.

Group sizes: 10-50

Typical behaviour: The movement through the water is slow and undulating. Pods may be seen resting motionless in the water and from a distance, look like logs. Will often allow boats to approach. Sometimes seen slapping their tails down against the surface of the water.

Confused with: May be confused with the minke whale. Head shape of the pilot is rounded not pointed and the flippers lack the distinctive white bands. The dorsal fin of the pilot is thick and centrally placed whereas that of the minke is fine, sharply pointed and noticeably nearer the tail.

GREY SEAL
(Halichoerus grypus)

Length: 2.5m (8ft)

ID features:
Colouration is highly variable with females being slightly lighter than males. They may appear grey, brown or black with dark mottling. The nostrils form a 'W' shape at the tip of the snout and are convex in shape giving individuals a distinct 'Roman' nose profile. Infants are covered with white fur for the first month of life.

Typical behaviour: Large groups often seen sunning themselves on rocks. The approach of a boat will generally cause them to take rapidly to the water. Once in the water, large, whiskery faces will pop up and stare back at their observers before rolling over to dive beneath the surface. Can sometimes be seen resting vertically in the water like corked bottles.

Confused with: The common seal (see below) and otters. In the water seals 'hang out' with a lazy unhurried attitude whereas otters tend to be swift and business-like in their movements.

COMMON SEAL
(Phoco vitulina)

Length: 1.5m (5ft)

ID features: Coloration can vary from grey to brown to black with mottling on the back. The muzzle is short, making the eyes appear large. The nostrils form a distinctive 'V' shape and the head is rounded. Pups have same coloration as adult.

Typical behaviour: Fast agile swimmers. They have an inquisitive nature and will often pop up close to boats. When on land individuals tend to be widely spaced preferring their own company to that of other group members.

Confused with: Grey seal and otters. Common seals are smaller than greys and have an almost dog like head with large soft eyes and a snub nose. If the animal can be seen observing a boat or person it is unlikely to be an otter. Generally otters are extremely shy and will vanish if disturbed, they are also much smaller and have a uniform brown coloration.

OTTER
(Lutra lutra)

Length: 1.2m (4ft)

ID features: Fur colour is medium to dark brown on the back with paler fur on the belly and a cream patch under the chin. The tail, used as a rudder when swimming, is long, stout and thick at the base. The ears are small and lie close to the head. Legs are short and powerful and all feet are webbed.

Typical behaviour: Graceful fluid movers both in and out of water. Normally extremely shy.

Confused with: Grey and common seals, also confused with mink. Otters are smaller than seals and can be distinguished by their shy behaviour and uniformly dark brown coat. Mink are similar in shape but much smaller than the otter. Mink have much darker coloration, at times appearing almost black. Their tails are fluffy and cylindrical whereas otters have a stout tail that tapers toward the end and when swimming flicks up out of the water prior to a dive. Mink, like seals, tend to be curious in the presence of humans, which otters are not.

MINK
(Mustela lutreola)

Length: 0.28-0.43m (1-2ft)

ID features: Uniformly dark brown fur which may appear black when wet. White spotting on the upper, and sometimes lower, lip. The ears are short and set close together. Long, bushy tail, short legs and partially webbed feet.

Typical behaviour: Fast and agile both in and out of the water. Generally nocturnal and solitary. Tend to be inquisitive, seldom missing the opportunity to sneak a glance at passers by. Highly efficient predators, being able to steal eggs from nests and catch anything from fish and crabs, to rabbits and birds. Will make a high pitched piping noise when alarmed.

Confused with: Most frequently otters (see above) but may also be confused with grey and/or common seals. The distinguishing feature is size.

DEEP WATER OFFSHORE SPECIES

HUMPBACK WHALE
(Megaptera novaengliae)

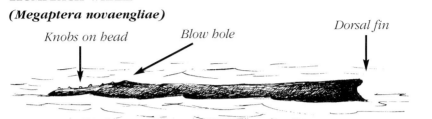

Knobs on head   *Blow hole*   *Dorsal fin*

Length: 11-15 (38-50ft) Sometimes referred to as 'clowns of the sea' as they are often seen jumping clear of the water, rolling on its surface or slapping their tails against it. They have a tall (3m) bushy blow, knobbly head and long, white, slender, flippers. Tail flukes, which have irregular white patterns, may be seen before a dive.

SPERM WHALE
(Physeter macrocephalus)

Length: 11-18 (36-59ft) Easy to identify by the angled bushy blow, from a single blow hole at front of head, and tail fluke which will be seen prior to a deep dive. The colossal head (almost one-third the animals' length) is blunt and rounded. The dorsal hump is two-thirds of the way down the back, which is slate grey in colour. May be seen in the deep waters off the continental shelf.

SEI WHALE
(Balaenoptera borealis)

Length: 9-24m (30-78ft). Cone shaped bushy blow (3m), whitish patch on head, and central ridge on snout. Very curved dorsal fin placed two-thirds of the way down a steely grey back.

FIN WHALE
(Balaenoptera physalus)

Length: 18m (60ft). Strong vertical bushy blow (4-6m high). Slender form with a dark, steely grey back, sometimes mottled. White underside. Curved dorsal fin, which points backwards, and is placed two-thirds of the way down back. The right hand jaw is white - very characteristic!

BLUE WHALE
(Balaenoptera musculus)

Length: 23-28m(75-90ft) The largest animal ever to have lived on earth, as big as a jumbo jet! Mottled greyish blue back, pale flippers. Tall (7.5m) blow, very small, slightly curved, dorsal fin placed three-quarters of the way down back. Extremely rare.

BASKING SHARK
(Cetorhinus maximus)

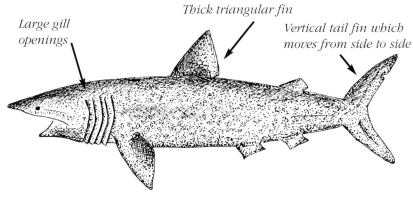

Large gill openings

Thick triangular fin

Vertical tail fin which moves from side to side

Length: 9-10m (20-24ft)

ID features: THE BASKING SHARK IS NOT A MARINE MAMMAL, IT IS A FISH! Uniformly slate grey though may sometimes appear almost black. Has a large thick triangular shaped dorsal fin placed two thirds of the way down the back. The tail fin, which stands vertically, is angular, pointed and curved slightly backwards, may also be seen. The snout, which has a conical tip, projects beyond the mouth. Gill openings, so large that they extend right around the neck, are clearly visible at close quarters.

Typical behaviour: Most often seen whilst feeding which they do by cruising along the surface of the water with a wide gaping mouth. The snout may be slightly above the water level. In this position the dorsal fin lies high out of the water and can be clearly seen. Little attention is paid to boats. May congregate in loose schools or pairs.

Confused with: Most cetaceans. Look for the presence of *two* fins (dorsal and tail), a large, slow, steady, moving bulk and, at close quarters, the gill openings.

GUIDELINES FOR WATCHING MARINE MAMMALS

To have the opportunity to watch any marine mammal in its natural environment is a remarkable gift but care must be taken to avoid disturbing or interfering with them. If watching from a boat the best way to enjoy an encounter is to allow the animals themselves to initiate the rendezvous. The need for sensitivity and respect when one is close to these magnificent animals can not be over-emphasised. The following guidelines were written for watching whales but are relevant to virtually all marine mammals. When watching marine mammals from a boat we strongly advise that these guidelines are adhered to but would like to point out that they are not exhaustive - if you are unsure whether or not your presence is disturbing the animals, leave the area quietly.

- Always keep a good look out - if you see whales, SLOW DOWN and avoid sudden changes in speed, direction or noise.

- Approach whales with caution and never from head-on. Keep the engine running to ensure both your manoeuvrability and that the whale can hear you.

- Never chase, encircle or overtake whales or cause groups to separate. Leave a good distance between the boat and the whale. If the boat gets too close the whale may become frightened and swim away. Remember that the best encounters occur when the whales themselves decide to approach you!

- Exercise extreme caution if mother/calf pairs or young whales are present - they are easily disturbed and more susceptible to collisions. Ideally leave them alone.

- If whales show any signs of becoming disturbed or alarmed move away slowly and keep away.

- If you observe another vessel enjoying an encounter with a whale, wait until they have moved out of the area before you approach.

- On some occasions whales will simply not be 'in the mood' to be approached. Don't put pressure on your skipper to get close on these occasions.

- If dolphins approach your vessel and start to bowride do not change course or speed simply continue as before and enjoy the encounter. However, if the dolphins change direction don't chase them.

- Dispose of fuel, oil, litter, food and other contaminants appropriately on the shore to avoid additional marine pollution.

These guidelines were taken from the 'Minke Whales and Whale Watching in the British Isles' leaflet produced by the International Fund for Animal Welfare. For further information on the International Whaling Commission's proposed general principles for whale watching, see International Whaling Commission 1996. Report of the Scientific Committee. Rep. Int. Whal. Commn. 46:56-58.

Model Marine Mammal

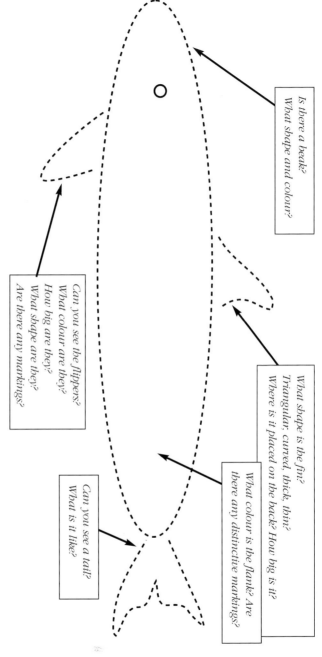

Is there a beak?
What shape and colour?

What shape is the fin?
Triangular, curved, thick, thin?
Where is it placed on the back? How big is it?

What colour is the flank? Are
there any distinctive markings?

Can you see the flippers?
What colour are they?
How big are they?
What shape are they?
Are there any markings?

Can you see a tail?
What is it like?

BEHAVIOUR:-

Activity? Bowriding, surfacing, feeding, jumping?
Where? Near the boat? Deep water? Near/far from shore?
How many? Large or small group?
Were there any seabirds present?